UC

D1199521

S

SEA SO BIG, SHIP SO SMALL

The Sailor's Prayer

Oh Lord,
Thy sea is so big
And my ship is so small,
Have mercy.

SEA SO BIG, SHIP SO SMALL

JEANNE BENDICK

Rand McNally & Company

New York • Chicago • San Francisco

FOREWORD

Every year millions of Americans, including many young people, throng our waterways as part of the ever-growing number of recreational boatmen. For the Coast Guard, as the chief United States agency for promoting maritime safety, this has meant an increasing emphasis on small boat safety to help prevent needless loss of life and property through boating accidents.

This book, written in simple, understandable terms for younger members of the small boat fraternity, serves admirably to acquaint all boatmen, both young and old, with the basic facts of small boat safety. It may be read with profit by all who participate in this healthful activity. In helping to spread the gospel of safe boating, this book should assist us materially in making boating an even safer activity than heretofore. In my opinion, the present volume is a significant contribution to the cause of safer recreational boating.

E. J. ROLAND
Admiral, U.S. Coast Guard
Commandant

To
Jean and Janice Grant

Thanks to
American Red Cross,
New York State Conservation Department,
  Division of Motor Boats,
Cornwall Miller of The Boating Industry,
and Robert Bendick, Senior and Junior,
for the material they made available,
and for their help and suggestions.

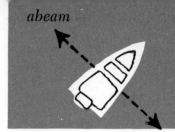
abeam

A SPECIAL LANGUAGE

Sometimes boating talk sounds like a new language, but it is a lot easier to learn. There are hundreds of words that are special to boating. Here are some that you should know.

ABEAM   *Amidships, or at a right angle to the boat*
ABOARD   *On, in, or into a boat*
AFT   *Toward the stern of a boat*
AHEAD   *Toward the bow*
AHOY!   *A nautical "Hello"*
ALL HANDS   *The whole crew*
AMIDSHIPS   *The middle of a boat*
ASTERN   *Toward the stern. Anything aft, whether in the boat or in the water is "astern."*

all hands

AYE   *"Yes," while aboard, or "I understand"*
BAIL   *To remove water from the boat by pumping or bailing*
BARNACLES   *Shellfish that cling to ships' bottoms (also to rocks, pilings, etc.)*

barnacles

BEARING   *The direction at which anything is seen*
BELAY   *To make fast, or sometimes to cancel an order*
BEND   *To fasten with a knot (also a kind of knot)*
BILGE   *The lower, inside part of the hull*
BOW   *The front of the boat*
BRIGHT WORK   *Natural, unpainted wood*
CALKING or CAULKING   *Forcing material between the planks of a boat to make the seams watertight*
CAN   *A cylinder-shaped buoy*
CAST OFF   *To untie mooring lines*
CHART   *A waterways map, giving all necessary information*

can

CHOCK   *A metal (or sometimes wood) piece for providing a fair-lead (see below)*

CLEAT   *A piece of metal or wood for making lines fast*

COCKPIT   *The sitting or steering space in the deck of a boat*

COMPASS   *Instrument for showing direction*

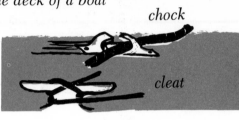
chock

COMPASS POINT   *A precise direction on the compass*

COURSE   *Direction in which boat is heading*

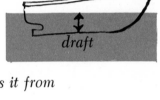
cleat

CRADLE   *A frame for holding a boat upright on land*

CURRENT   *The horizontal movement of water*

DAVY JONES' LOCKER   *The bottom of the sea*

DRAFT   *The depth of water needed to float a boat*

DRY ROT   *A fungus that causes wood to decay and come apart*

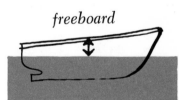
draft

EBB   *Outgoing tide*

FAIR-LEAD   *Serves as a guide for the line and keeps it from chafing*

FATHOM   *A nautical measure equal to 6 feet*

FENDERS   *Bumpers placed along a boat to keep it from rubbing or bumping something outside*

FITTING OUT   *Getting the boat ready to put in the water for a season's sailing*

FLOOD   *Incoming tide*

freeboard

FORE   *Forward of amidships*

FREEBOARD   *The height of a boat's sides, amidships, from the water line up*

GALLEY   *Where the cooking is done*

GEAR   *Equipment and supplies aboard*

HAIL   *To call another boat*

ahoy!

HEAD   *Toilet compartment*

HEADSEA   *Big waves in front of the boat*

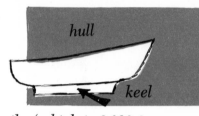
headsea

HELM   *The steering wheel or tiller*

HITCH   *A way of fastening rope*

HP   *Short for horsepower*

HULL   *The body of a boat*

hull

keel

KEEL   *The "backbone" of a boat, running fore and aft along the bottom*

KNOT   *A unit of speed equal to one nautical mile (which is 6,080.2 feet) an hour. Boatmen never say, "knots per hour," just "knots." Knot also means to bend a line.*

LEEWARD   *On the side away from the wind*

leeward side

wind

LEEWAY   *The drift of a boat caused by the wind or current*

LIST   *The leaning of a boat toward one side*

LOG   *An instrument for finding a ship's speed*

LOG BOOK   *A diary of happenings aboard*

MATE   *Next in command to the Captain*

NUN   *A buoy, tapering at the top*

nun

PAINTER   *A boat's bow rope, used for making her fast*

PITCH   *Fore or aft movement as the bow and stern rise and fall in the waves*

PORT   *The left side of a boat when you are facing forward*

ROLL   *The sideward rocking of a boat caused by wind and waves*

port side

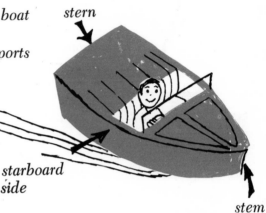

RUDDER *A steering device attached, below the water, to the stern or rudder post*

SOUND *To find out the depth of the water*

STARBOARD *The right side of a boat when you are facing forward*

STEM *The upright post that supports the bow*

STERN *The after end of a boat*

rudder

stern

starboard
side

stem

STOW *To put away*

TIDE *The regular rise and fall of water, caused by the gravitational pull of the moon and sun*

TILLER *A handle that turns a boat's rudder, or an outboard's motor*

TRANSOM *The flat, after end of a boat*

TRIM *To arrange the weight of a boat so it balances efficiently*

UNDER WAY *Moving through the water, not moored or anchored*

WAKE *The track of moving water behind a boat*

windward
side

wake

WINDWARD *On the side toward the wind*

Sailing terms are different too. You'll find some of these on pages 26-30.

SEA SO BIG, SHIP SO SMALL

All good sailors respect the sea.

The sea, to a sailor, doesn't have to mean the ocean. It could be a big lake or a small one, a river, a bay, or a sound —any water he boats on. But whatever water he sails, a good boatman is always alert. Being a sailor is a little like being a lion tamer. No matter how skillful you are, or how well you know your lion's moods, you never really let down your guard.

No one ever knows a lion—or the sea—so well that he can't be surprised.

But you can know your boat well.

Boats are a little like people. In some ways they are all alike. But as you get to know boats you will notice that even boats that look exactly alike, and are made exactly alike, don't always behave that way.

One will turn more easily one way than another. Each boat will take the waves differently. Some will be harder to handle going into the waves than others; some won't like a following sea.

It's easier to get along with your friends if you know their likes and dislikes, and the same is true of boats. Be sensitive to the way your boat behaves. The better you know it, the better you'll get along together.

You can learn a lot by watching an expert handle a boat, but you have to get the feel of it yourself, too. You need plenty of practice, with an expert aboard. Boating is not only safer but a lot more fun if you do it right.

And some time your life might even depend on your knowing your boat's strong or weak points.

WHAT IS A GOOD BOAT?

A good boat is sound. It has no leaks, no rotten or broken places. It is clean and shipshape from stem to stern. All gear is in good order.

A good boat is one you can handle, alone if necessary.

A good boat is always safe. It is one you can keep in good repair without having to let anything go until you have the time or money to fix it.

It is right for the water you sail in.

If you do your boating in shallow water or rocky places, you need a boat with a bottom like this

If you sail in deep water you can have a deeper keel.

A good boat for you is the one that suits your needs.

Do you have to bring your boat onto a beach?

Do you have to trailer it or carry it?

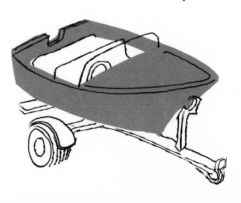

Do you use your boat for fishing?
or water skiing?
or cruising?

A good boat is different for each of these things.

CANOES are good boats for lakes or quiet rivers, but too tippy for rough water. A canoe is light enough to carry on top of a car. Some have a stern that will hold an outboard.

DINGHIES and PRAMS are good beginner boats, but they are not for rough water either. They are usually from 7 to 12 feet long, and are light enough to carry on top of a car. Two people—three at most—are a good load for a pram or dink. Prams and dinks are easy to row, can carry outboards of up to 3 horsepower, and some can be rigged for sailing.

ROWBOATS are bigger—up to 18 feet—and are more rugged. They can carry more people and are safe in rougher water. Depending on its size, a rowboat can carry an outboard of up to 10 horsepower.

dinghy

rowboat

11

utility

UTILITY BOATS look something like rowboats, but they are not built for rowing. Utilities are generally used for fishing or for dock service. Some are small and light. Some are big enough to be safe for fishing in open water. Depending on its size, a utility can carry an outboard of from 5 to 50 horsepower.

runabout

RUNABOUTS are the sports cars of the boat family. Because they are fast, they are good for getting from place to place, and best for water skiing. Some have inboards, but most have outboard motors.

OUTBOARD CRUISERS are the smallest of the big boats. They usually have bunks, a galley, and a head. Even big outboard cruisers can be carried on a trailer and stored in your own yard. But outboard cruisers, and all the bigger ones, are family boats. The most you could be is a good first mate!

If a SAILBOAT is the boat for you, see page 26.

outboard cruiser

BUYING A BOAT

Whatever kind of boat you get, remember that you have to support it! You have to keep it shipshape. You will need equipment and a place to keep it. If it's a motor boat you will have to buy fuel. You will want insurance. Count all these things in your budget.

A new boat is usually a family boat. If it's a small boat that the family has agreed to take turns using, be fair about sharing the time *and* doing your share of the work.

If this is your first boat, it's a fine idea to look for a good used boat of the kind you want. But don't expect to get a big bargain. A well-constructed, well-cared-for boat doesn't depreciate in value, and usually it has improvements that a new boat hasn't. If you're inexperienced, be sure to take an expert with you to check for hidden defects.

Maybe you want to build your own boat. There are excellent boat-kits of almost every type. These can save you a lot of money, IF you're a good do-it-yourself man. And building a boat is an exciting project.

Don't buy any boat without an expert—or a committee of experts—to help you!

But whether you buy your boat new, or used, or build it yourself, whether it's yours or the family's, share your boat. That's half the fun!

13

KEEPING YOUR BOAT SHIPSHAPE

Be sure your boat contains flotation material—plastic foam blocks—and *never* tamper with, or remove, any of this material. With flotation material a boat will float even if it fills with water, and even if it turns over. But the boat must be in good shape!

Never leave shore in a leaky boat.

If you notice something that needs fixing while you are under way, return to shore immediately and fix it right away. Don't wait until next time. You may forget, or be in such a hurry to get afloat that you're tempted to skip it.

Put aside real time for big jobs, even if it means staying in port a day.

Some jobs should be done by professionals. Don't try

to calk a really bad leak
to repair a broken plank or a broken rib
to mend a large hole in a plastic boat
to make major motor repairs (unless
you are a real whiz at motors.)

BEFORE YOU STORE YOUR BOAT IN THE WINTER

Clean it thoroughly.
Be sure the ropes and lines are dry and properly stored
(see pages 48-49).
Clean and grease the motor.
Check the boat and make a note of all the jobs to be done,
and any improvements you want to make while they are
fresh in your mind.

WHEN YOU TAKE YOUR BOAT OUT IN THE SPRING

Check it from stem to stern, from keel to topmast, inside
and out, topside and below. Check any wiring. Check steering
cables and rods. Check your motor, and oil it according to the
manufacturer's directions.

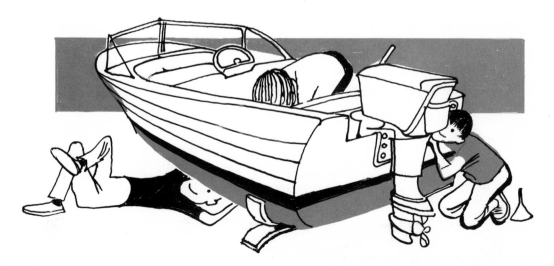

*To do a good paint job
you must*
1. *sandpaper*
2. *wash down*
3. *use a good marine paint*
4. *use a good brush*
5. *flow paint on*

With the boat on dry land, it is easy to examine every part. Tap, pound, sniff, jab, and look. If anything needs fixing, do it now. It is cheaper and safer.

Now is the time to paint. Always use marine paint on your boat.

Did you scrape the barnacles off the bottom when you took it out of the water? They make your boat sluggish. If you waited, do it now. Then use an anti-fouling bottom paint, and it's better to put your boat in the water before this paint is dry.

CHECKLIST FOR A SHIPSHAPE BOAT

Are the fastenings—the screws and rivets that hold the boat together—in good condition? Or are they rusty or wobbly?

Are the fittings all tight, and do you polish them occasionally?

Is the paint in good condition? Water makes bare wood rotten and unpainted steel rusty.

Is any bright work varnished? You have to do this job several times a season.

Are the seams tight and waterproof? Fix any cracks with calking compound and a putty knife.

YOUR MOTOR

More than half the pleasure boats in the United States are outboard motor boats. But whether you have an inboard or an outboard engine you should be familiar with it, and know how it pushes the boat.

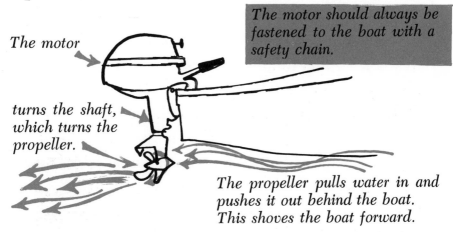

The motor

turns the shaft, which turns the propeller.

The motor should always be fastened to the boat with a safety chain.

The propeller pulls water in and pushes it out behind the boat. This shoves the boat forward.

You should know what happens to the bow and the stern when you turn the wheel or swing the outboard handle.

A boat steers mainly from the stern.

If you turn the bow a little to the left, the stern swings much farther to the right.

An outboard motor is easy to run, easy to take care of, and safe if you understand it and if it's the right size for your boat.

Every manufacturer prints a manual, telling you the best way to take care of the engines he makes. Even if you have an old motor, the manufacturer will be glad to send you a manual that tells about it, and it's a handy thing to have.

If the motor is too big, the bow will go up and the stern will go down. In a rough sea, water coming in over the stern can swamp your boat.

If the motor is too small, the boat will be hard to steer, but too small is better than too big!

Here is a guide to motorboat sizes as recommended by the Outboard Boating Club of America. The numbers down the side of the chart are the sizes of boats. Find your size by multiplying the length of the boat by the width at the stern.

The numbers across the top are engine sizes by horsepower.

When you have your boat size, look down the line until you meet the curve, then look up for the engine size.

Remember that this is only a guide. Other things have to be considered, too, so when you think you have figured out the size of the motor for your boat, have it checked by an expert.

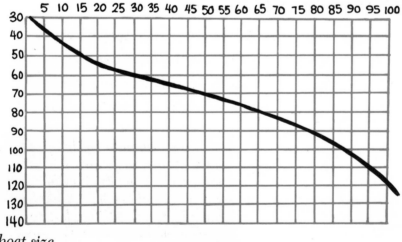

engine size in horsepower

boat size in feet

multiply width at stern by length of boat

18

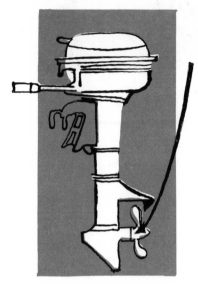

shear pin

Behind the propeller, here, is the shear pin. If the propeller hits an obstruction, the shear pin is supposed to break. When the shear pin breaks, the propeller stops, which keeps it from being damaged. But the boat won't go anywhere if the propeller isn't turning, so always keep a couple of extra shear pins in your tool kit, just in case! If you unscrew the propeller, you will see the broken shear pin. Knock it out and replace it with one of your spares.

If you can't bring the whole motor into the boat, be very careful not to drop any parts overboard!

FUEL

Some outboards work best on a mixture of marine gas and oil. The manual for your motor will tell you what mixture is best for you. If you have to mix, use your spare gas can, which should be a *safety approved tank.* Close the cap and shake well before pouring the mixture into the motor tank. Use a strainer funnel, because sand or dirt can ruin your motor. And be careful not to get water in.

Check your fuel system and connections to be sure everything is tight and free from leaks.

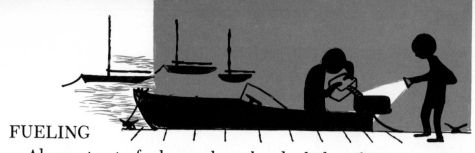

FUELING

Always try to fuel your boat by daylight. If you ever fuel in the dark, use a flashlight and *never* an open flame. Don't let anyone smoke on or near the boat when you are fueling.

GASOLINE IS VERY EXPLOSIVE

If any spills, wipe it up at once. (And get rid of that oily rag as soon as possible, on shore.)

Be sure the spout from the gas can or hose is touching your fuel pipe or tank before the gas is poured, and keep them in contact all through pouring. This prevents static electricity from making a spark and causing an explosion.

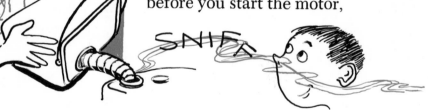

Never fill your tank to the brim because gasoline expands when it is heated.

After filling your tank, put the top on as tightly as you can. And then, before you start the motor,

Don't start until all the gasoline vapor is gone.

If your motor is inboard, ventilate any closed areas before you start it. Gasoline vapor settles and stays. It can be ignited by any spark. Keep your safety can of spare gas away from the engine and where it can get fresh air.

BEFORE YOU LEAVE THE DOCK

Never take a boat out without saying where you are going and when you expect to be back.

If you're the captain, you're the boss, but remember, you also have all the responsibility!

The skipper is first into the boat, but before you step aboard, check to be sure the mooring lines are secure, so the boat won't slip away as you step in.

Never jump into a boat. Step aboard as close to midship as you can, keeping low and steady. (If you are moored bow first, step aboard over the bow.) Once you are in, you can steady the boat for other passengers when they come aboard.

Don't carry things while boarding—you need both hands. Have someone hand them in afterward, or leave them within your reach on the dock.

Before anyone else boards, pump or bail out any water in the boat. Is there a lot?

It *might* be rain.

But it *might* be a leak, and under power a little crack can become a large split. Make sure at the dock.

If you take your motor ashore each time, don't try to hitch it onto the boat directly from the dock. People lose more motors that way! Pass it into the boat first,

fasten the safety chain,

then put the motor securely in place.

When all the gear is passed in and stored out of the way so it won't slide around, the passengers can come aboard. Remember, DON'T OVERLOAD. "One more doesn't matter" are famous last words.

Be sure the combined weight of passengers and gear is not too much for the boat. You can generally tell by looking.

When you are painting your boat, paint a line one-third of the distance up from the keel as a rough guide. If that line is under water when you are under way, you are overloaded. Even freighters have these lines painted on their sides. Remember this is just a guide—and only for protected waters.

EQUIPMENT CHECKLIST

There are some things every boat should have, whether it is a dink or a yacht.

Never leave shore without these things.

Check them every time.

AN APPROVED LIFE SAVER FOR EVERY PASSENGER ✓

Stow these out of the way, but in easy reach. *Never* keep them in a locked compartment. Don't sit on them, and dry them out after every use. Non-swimmers should wear life preservers that fit.

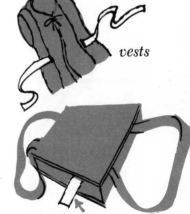

vests

"approved" tag

Life preservers can be safety approved cushions
(be sure the straps are secure)

or rings

FIRE EXTINGUISHER

This should be dry chemical, carbon dioxide, or foam (some other kinds are not approved).

TWO DOCKING LINES and AT LEAST ONE SPARE COIL OF ROPE, 100 FEET OR MORE

AT LEAST ONE ANCHOR and LINE (larger boats should have two)

LARGE FLASHLIGHT WITH GOOD BATTERIES (check them often)

OARS or PADDLES

TOOL KIT (with replacement shear pins)

FIRST AID KIT

PUMP or BAILER

HORN or WHISTLE (audible for two miles)

COMPASS

CHART OF THE AREA (in a waterproof chart envelope)

DRINKING WATER

EXTRA FUEL IN A SAFETY TANK

FENDERS

And to keep the boat looking shipshape, you should have a CLEANING KIT: a large sponge, a scrub brush, cleaning powder in a jar or plastic container (cardboard ones get soggy), and any special cleaning material your boat needs.

Now take a final check.

A good captain assigns a job to each member of his crew.

Is the boat trim? (That means passengers and gear are well balanced.)

Is all boat and safety equipment aboard?

Is everyone wearing an approved life preserver?

Have you left word where you are going?

Has the weather changed?

Is the propeller clear of weeds, rocks, or debris?

Is the motor shut-off valve open?

Now you can start your motor. When it is running smoothly, but before you untie the lines, look around. All clear?

Then cast off, signal one long horn blast, and pull away.

Coil your lines and stow them out of the way.

sloop   *ketch*   *yawl*   *schooner*

SAILBOATS ARE DIFFERENT

If you know a little about motors, and can steer and use your common sense, you could probably get into a motorboat and go. But sailboats are different. You can't just get into a sailboat and sail. Sailing takes skill and knowledge.

If you have a sailboat you should know how the wind moves it; how to handle your tiller, sheets, and sails to make it go in any direction; how to slow it down, stop it, or straighten it up if it's heeling too far.

Sailboats look different from one another above the waterline, with many kinds of sails, rigs, and masts in different positions. They are different below the water too, and that difference is important when you are choosing a sailboat for your needs.

Some sailboats have a heavy, fixed keel that goes deep in the water and can't be moved. These are very stable.

Some sailboats are centerboarders. They have a keel board, without a weight, that can be raised in shallow water and lowered in deep or rough water.

A catamaran has no keel or centerboard. It sits on top of the water and is a sailing platform with a hull on each side to steady it.

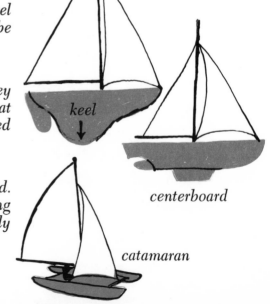

keel

centerboard

catamaran

Which is best for you?

If you sail in deep water, and have a place to moor or dock your boat, then you can have a fixed keel. Large sailboats usually have a fixed keel.

If you have to bring it into shallow water, you can have a centerboard or a catamaran.

If you have to bring your boat through the surf or onto a beach, a catamaran is best.

If you do your sailing only in a bathing suit, and don't mind tipping, you can have a sailboat that is almost a sailing surfboard with a finlike centerboard that can be raised and lowered.

If you think you might want to race your boat, check before you buy to see what boats race in your area. Different classes are popular in different areas, and boats race with their own class. Once you have learned the fundamentals, racing is the best way to become an expert sailor.

Most small sailboats are *sloop rigged*. They have a *mainsail* (say "mains'l"), and another sail forward which is called a *jib* if it is small, a *jenny* if it is larger.

Some small sailboats, like the sailing surfboard kind, have only one sail.

On a sailboat, the lines that raise, lower, and support the sails are called *halyards*. The lines that control the sails are called *sheets*.

A sailboat sails because the wind is pushing against the sails. The wind can be behind or on either side, but it cannot sail straight into the wind.

If the wind is coming from here and that's where you want to sail, you have to *tack*, or sail a zigzag course, so the wind can push on the sails from the side.

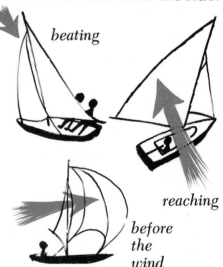

When the wind is coming from here, the sails have to be almost parallel to the boat, or close-hauled. *This is called* beating.

When the wind is abeam, the sail is extended and the boat is reaching. *Reaching is the fastest point of sail.*

When the wind is behind, the sail is at right angles to the boat, and the boat is before the wind. *When you see boats with the big, balloon-like sails called* spinnakers *up, they are sailing before the wind.*

beating

reaching

before the wind

When a good wind is pushing hard against the sails from either side, the boat will *heel* over, sometimes until one rail is in the water and the bottom is showing. This is not dangerous *if* the skipper knows his job. When a sailboat heels, the crew sits on the high side to trim it. Sometimes they "hike" way out over the water.

The crew is "hiking" to trim the boat.

*Starboard tack
has right of way.*

*Leeward boat
has right of way.*

A sailboat under sail generally has right of way over all motor boats *unless* its motor is on too. Then it is considered a motor boat.

A sailboat on a starboard tack, which means the wind is coming from the starboard side, has right of way over a sailboat on a port tack.

If two sailboats are on the same tack the *leeward* boat (the one farthest from the wind) has right of way.

A sailboat sailor has to pay even more attention to wind and weather than a motorboatman, because he is absolutely dependent on them.

If the wind looks more than you can handle safely, DON'T GO OUT. Unless you know what to do, a strong wind can knock a sailboat down. If you are out and the wind picks up strongly, reduce sail.
You can *reef in* the main (tie or roll it to make it smaller), or take down the jib, or sail on your jib alone.

A strong, steady wind isn't very hard to handle. It's the sudden gusts that are dangerous.

*Winds over 10 knots are
for experienced sailors.*

In a gust, either turn the bow FAST into the wind (a sailboat can't sail right into the wind), or ease the sheet—let out the line that is holding the sail tight. When the sail is loose, the wind can't push against it.

Because a sailboat can't find shelter as fast as a power boat can, allow extra time to get to harbor if the weather is threatening. If a storm comes up suddenly, *take down sail* and ride it out. If you have a centerboard, put it all the way down. The deeper a keel or centerboard is, the steadier a boat is in the water. (That's one reason why small sailboats are safer in the open sea than small power boats.)

If your anchor can reach bottom, anchor on as much line as you have. If the water is too deep to anchor, a sea anchor will steady your boat. Tie anything that floats (sailboat cover, life preserver) to a bow line and let it out into the water. This will help hold the bow into the wind.

Even if your boat swamps and fills with water, STAY WITH IT. You may feel as if you are sitting in the bathtub, but even if it is filled to the rail, a shipshape boat will float.

To "ride it out"
1. *take down sail*
2. *lower centerboard if you have one*
3. *put out a sea anchor*

and STAY WITH IT!

ROWBOATS AND CANOES

A rowboat or a canoe, even without a motor, is a good first boat. Either one can teach you a lot about boats.

Rowboats are good fishing and picnic boats, because they are steady and have very little draft. You can get in close to rocks or shore and they are easy to beach.

Because you have to sit backward in a rowboat, turn around occasionally to be sure you're not rowing into anything.

Keep your rowboat as shipshape as if it were a yacht.

And remember, because *you* are the motor, don't get so far from shore that you can't get in easily without getting exhausted.

Most canoes are not as steady as rowboats, so they are not for rough water, but wonderful for lakes and quiet rivers. If you are paddling alone, sit amidships and change your paddle from side to side as you need to change direction.

A non-swimmer should never use a canoe.

If your canoe should tip, it's easy to flip it back over. Then hoist yourself back in, amidship.

If you have a rowboat or a canoe you should be able to handle your oars or paddle in rough water or smooth, with a partner or alone.

Pull the canoe toward you and put one arm on the far side. Then hoist yourself in.

Rocking the canoe from side to side will get most of the water out.

31

Sneakers save boats and people—but not if the soles are smooth.

BOAT MANNERS

Courtesy afloat isn't just politeness. It makes boating safer and pleasanter for everybody.

Aboard any boat, from a pram to a battleship, everyone obeys the Captain. Since he is responsible for everybody aboard, he must have the authority to give the orders. Boats are not run by committees, so if you are a passenger, obey without arguing. And if you are the Captain, don't let your command go to your head! Your crew may mutiny and put you ashore!

A good boatman shows his consideration in many ways.

He gives whatever help he can to any boat that is disabled or aground.

He never speeds past swimmers, rowboats, water skiers, fishermen.

He slows down in areas where other boats are docked.

He never goes aboard another boat unless invited.

He never throws trash in the water. (Even if you sink cans and bottles they can wash ashore.) Keep a bag aboard for your litter.

He slows down and stays clear of sailboats. If they are racing, he keeps clear of the entire fleet. It is impossible to run through without putting somebody at a disadvantage.

He keeps his wake low when passing other boats, floats, or docks. (This is not just good manners. You are responsible for any damage caused by your wake.)

A good boatman is helpful and cooperative. He uses his common sense.

RULES OF THE ROAD

"Rules of the Road" are as important on the water as traffic rules are on the highway. They are made to prevent accidents. They are different in different waters, so be sure you know the local rules.

But don't learn just the rules that apply to you and your boat and then stick to them, no matter what! You have to add a dash of courtesy and a lot of common sense. On the highway, everybody knows the rules—you can't get a driver's license unless you do. But you may cross the path of a slap-happy boatman who doesn't know anything about the rules of the road. Then your job is to do whatever is sensible to avoid an accident.

Always be ready to lend a hand to a fellow boatman in trouble, even if that just means standing by until other help comes.

There aren't many speed limits on the water, just those posted in harbors or anchorages. But you are *always* responsible for any damage caused by the wake of your boat. This means damage to people, docks, floats, boats or anything on them, whether there is a speed limit posted or not.

You are always responsible for your wake.

Most rules of the road tell you who has the right of way and how to signal. Water is not like a highway where cars going in certain directions have their own lanes. Afloat, you will meet boats coming from all directions and going anywhere.

Some boats have the right of way over others.

Sailboats under sail have the right of way.

Sailboats under sail, rowboats and canoes, usually have the right of way over motorboats. If you are in a motorboat it's up to you to get out of the way, because your boat is easier to maneuver. When you meet sailboats, rowboats, or canoes, keep clear and pass astern.

Generally, it's a good idea to give the right of way to any boat that is less maneuverable and requires deep water. While technically you might have the right of way over an ocean liner or a freighter, don't put the captain to the test!

Fishing boats with nets out, and tugs pulling barges, always have the right of way.

Common sense is important too!

But most of the boats you meet will be other motorboats. This is how you tell who has the right of way.

If the other boat is anywhere in this area, from your point of view, he has the right of way. You are called the BURDENED VESSEL, and you must get out of his way.

You must get out of his way

you

You must hold course and speed

you

If the other boat is anywhere in this area, from your point of view, you have the right of way. You are the PRIVILEGED VESSEL.

Can you see that the boat to starboard has the right of way when boats meet?

The burdened vessel has the responsibility of getting out of the way, but the privileged vessel has a responsibility too. He must hold his course and speed until the other boat is clear.

If two boats are meeting this way, both turn to starboard and pass port side to port side. But if they are a safe distance apart, like this, they can pass starboard to starboard.

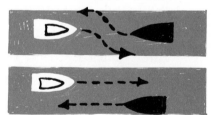

If there is any doubt, don't pass until you are sure of what the other captain is going to do.

IMPORTANT SIGNALS TO KNOW

short blasts: toot! I am turning to starboard
toot! toot! I am turning to port
toot! toot! toot! I am in reverse
toot! toot! toot! toot! (or more) DANGER!

PASSING SIGNALS

Cabin cruisers and other larger boats always use passing signals. Often small boats don't, but it is a good idea to know and use them. If your boat has no horn, you can get a very loud one attached to an aerosol can. It should be part of your boat equipment anyway.

Boats passing port to port, like this, each sound one blast.

Boats passing starboard to starboard each sound two blasts.

If you are overtaking another boat, he has the right of way. But you can't expect him to hold his course and speed unless he knows you are there, so signal.

1 blast: I am passing to starboard.

2 blasts: I am passing to port.

If it is unsafe to pass, he will give the danger signal, 4 short blasts. Then you must wait for a signal to pass.
1 blast. Pass me to starboard
2 blasts. Pass me to port. Returning the same signal shows that you understand.

long blasts: 1 each minute in fog, or any poor visibility
1 when leaving dock, or when approaching a bend in a river or channel
1 continuous blast—HELP!

37

NAVIGATION AIDS

Buoys and Lights

Buoys and lights are the road signs on water.

Buoys mark channels where the water is safe. The red buoy marks one side of the channel and the black buoy marks the other. Between them is the road.

When you are going out of a harbor, the red buoys should be on your left. When you are coming in, the red buoys should be on your right. If you remember these three R's, you'll never make a mistake: RED
RIGHT
RETURN

A black and white striped buoy marks the middle of a channel. It means "Pass close to, on either side."

All black buoys have odd numbers and all red buoys have even numbers. When you are using a chart, you can locate every buoy exactly by its number, which shows you just where you are. Number 1 is always the farthest buoy out to sea, and the numbers get bigger as you get into the harbor.

If you miss a number when you are coming into an unfamiliar harbor, take a good look around for it. The channel may take a sharp bend, and you could find yourself aground.

In a narrow channel, always keep to the right. Never anchor in a channel, and, except in a real emergency, never tie onto a buoy.

Buoys have different names.

This is a can.

This is a nun.

This is a spar.

This is a lighted bell.

A white spar shows an anchorage.

Black and white marks a fish net.

Many buoys are lighted at night. Red buoys have red or white lights. Black buoys have green or white lights. Mid-channel buoys always have white lights. If the buoys on one side of the channel are white, those on the other side will be red or green.

The lights on some buoys are steady, some are flashing, and some are occulting, going on and off, with the "on" time as long as, or longer than, the "off" time. The characteristics of every buoy's light are marked on your chart, so you can tell which one you are seeing at night.

Some buoys have bells or gongs, whistles or trumpets, so you can hear them when you can't see them.

unlighted bell, black

BONG

WHEE WHEE

unlighted whistle, red

steady light

flashing light

quick flashing light

occulting light

If you can't get a plastic chart of your area, keep yours in a plastic envelope.

CHARTS

The color, shape, and number of a buoy help you to find your exact location when you look at a chart. You should have a chart of your boating area, even if it's a familiar one. Never, never sail in unfamiliar waters without a chart.

If you do your boating on smaller lakes or rivers that are not charted, you could have an interesting time making your own.

A chart is much more fun to read than a map. It tells you everything you need to know about the waters you are sailing.

These symbols mean the same thing on every chart.

The numbers tell how deep the water is at *low tide*, in feet or fathoms (the chart says which).

lighthouse
buoy (N means nun, C means can, S means spar)
black buoy   red buoy
lighted buoy (Fl G "3" means: Number 3 buoy, flashing a green light)
light
channel (The depth of the channel and the date it was measured are marked, because channels shift.)
rocky ledges
rocks awash (at any tide)
submerged rocks

gravel and rocky bottoms (important to know when you anchor)
salt marsh
submerged wreck, dangerous to navigation
sunken wreck, not dangerous
lightship  2-masted lightship
whirlpool
anchorage
bridge (Numbers show height above water at high tide)
railroad

The compass rose shows which direc-
    tion is which on the chart

The star on a compass rose shows
true north. The arrow shows magnetic north, which is where your
compass points.

How many things can you see on this
chart that would be important to
know if you were sailing into this
harbor for the first time?

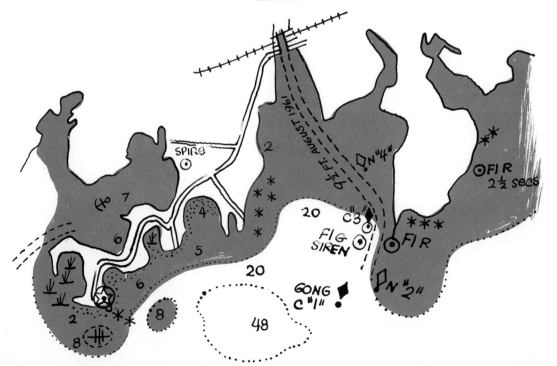

There are 32 points on the compass and 96 quarter points. North, East, South and West are called the cardinal points.

YOUR COMPASS

You should always have a compass aboard your boat, and know how to use it. Maybe you won't use your compass every day, but you would have to depend on it in darkness or in fog, or in planning a course from one harbor to another.

Your compass should be mounted permanently in your boat, where you can see it when you are steering, and should be away from the motor and any magnetic or electrical equipment.

To be a good captain, you need the rules of the road.

To be a good pilot, you should know exactly where you are at all times. You should be able to plot a course from one place to another and stay on it, by using your compass, reading your chart, and knowing your buoys and lights.

When you chart a course, lay it out on your chart in pencil or colored tape, like this. Mark the headings from your compass rose; then follow them on your compass.

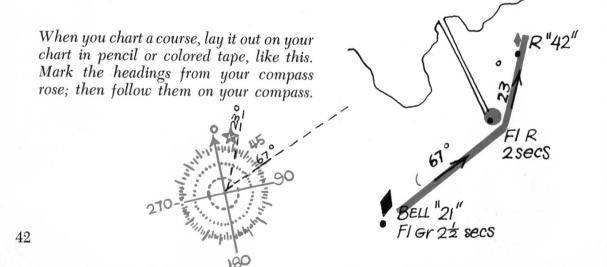

WEATHER

No good sailor is ever careless about the weather.

Bad weather and small boats don't mix. Strong winds make rough water, which can swamp your boat. Water carries lightning over great distances. And if you need help in bad weather, there isn't anyone around to give it. Everybody else is at home.

This is important enough to repeat. Always make a weather check before you take your boat out. Listen to the forecast on the radio. This will give you another clue, too. Sharp static means a thunderstorm is in the area.

Look for warning flags and lights.

A red pennant flying from any dock, flagpole, or Coast Guard station is a small craft warning. It means STAY ASHORE.

This is a gale warning.

This is a full gale warning.

This is a hurricane warning.

Even if the weather looks great, when they are flying, STAY ASHORE.

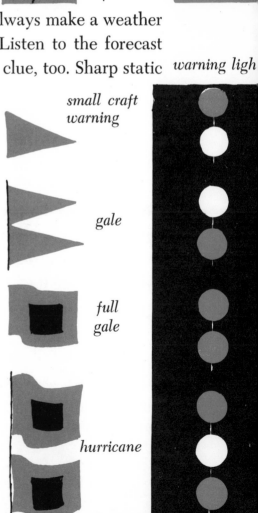

warning ligh[ts]

small craft warning

gale

full gale

hurricane

Sometimes it is too rough for small boats to be out even before the small craft warning is up. Maybe, at your anchorage, you can post a signal of your own to show winds over 10 knots. Small craft warnings go up at 18 knots, which is more than a small outboard can manage safely.

Learn to be your own weather expert. A sudden storm may develop even on a clear day, so keep alert for changes.

Weather generally moves from west to east. When you see clouds building up in the west, you can be pretty sure they are heading your way.

Watch for shifts in the wind. They usually mean a change in the weather.

A very red sky at sunrise generally means bad weather on the way. A gray or lavender sky means fair weather.

Do you have a barometer?
When the needle rises, the air pressure is high, the clouds are high, and the weather will be good.
When the needle falls, the air pressure is low. It pushes the clouds close to earth and the weather is bad.

Get to know these clouds:

CUMULUS—scattered, light, fluffy—mean good weather.

cumulus

cirrus

alto-cumulus mass into

cumulo-nimbus, or thunderheads

strato-cumulus

stratus

CIRRUS clouds won't bother you either. They are very high, very fast-moving ice crystals.

ALTOCUMULUS mean a thunderstorm when they really start massing. Get ashore fast. The water is the worst place to be in a thunderstorm.

STRATOCUMULUS, when they get very thick, mean bad weather.

STRATUS clouds almost always mean rain. But they make the day so dull and cloudy that you probably won't want to take your boat out anyway.

A thin, brown haze on the horizon is fog coming in.

A dirty, smudgy cloudline on the horizon is a squall on the way.

If you like to plan ahead, the weather map in your newspaper will give you a good idea of what kind of weather to expect in the next few days. Remember, weather usually moves from west to east.

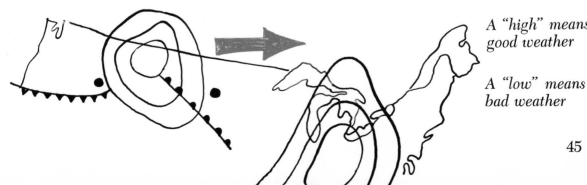

A "high" means good weather

A "low" means bad weather

45

WIND, TIDE, AND CURRENT

A boat isn't like a car. It doesn't have brakes to stop it. Water isn't like a road. A road stands still, but water is always moving. Sometimes it moves with the boat, which makes the boat go faster. Sometimes it moves against the boat, which slows it down.

Water moving in one direction is called a current.

Sometimes currents are caused by the wind.

Sometimes they are caused by the tide coming in or going out. If you live in a coastal area, you should be familiar with the tides there. Your local newspaper prints tide tables every day, which show you the times of high and low tides. Then you can see when the water will be high or low. You can see when the current will be strong going out and coming in. If the tidal currents in your area are strong, it's a good idea, if possible, to be with them, instead of bucking them.

Some places have special currents, always moving in one direction. Get to know any currents peculiar to your boating area.

Whenever you are in a current, whether you are going with it or against it, you cannot control your boat unless it is going faster than the current is. This does not mean that you should speed. When you go too fast, you are not in control of your boat either. No brakes, remember!

Strong current can stop your boat, give it a free ride, or push it sideways.

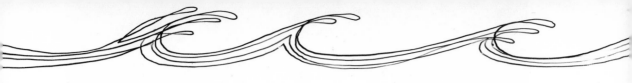

Wind affects the water too. It can make waves that push you from the front, or back, or sides.

Handling a boat in strong winds or current is tricky.

You must allow *leeway*.

This means that if you are going this way

and the wind is blowing from here

(or there is a strong current from here) you will have to steer a little this way to stay on course.

Otherwise the wind and current, or either one, will put you off course like this and you won't even realize it. Giving yourself leeway will keep you on course.

Learning to handle your boat in wind and current is basic to good seamanship.

There are a number of great and famous currents, and *prevailing* winds (always blowing in the same direction) in the world. Some time you might be interested in finding out how they have affected civilization, and even life itself on our planet.

When the sun, moon, and earth are in a line, the tides are higher.

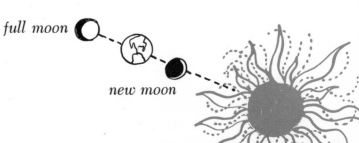

full moon

new moon

ROPE, LINES, AND KNOTS

Boatmen say that it is impossible to have too much line aboard a boat. You need at least two mooring lines—one fore, one aft. You need an anchor line at least six to eight times longer than the deepest water you anchor in. You need at least one utility line—100 feet long or more.

Buy the best line you can afford. Your lines keep your boat and you safe. If you take care of them, they will last for years. Keep them dry, coiled, and free of knots and kinks. Stow them in a dry place with plenty of fresh air.

hang looped line on a cleat

Coiling lines flat, like this, is the best way to keep them, but that isn't always practical on a small boat. Here is another good way to keep your rope aboard.

Clean mud, dirt, and grease off your lines.

Don't let them drag or rub continuously.

A chafeguard will protect rope in a place where it rubs a lot. You can buy rubber ones, or make them yourself out of tape, like this.

rubber chafe guard

tape chafe guard

It's a good idea to have chocks on your boat, fore and aft. They provide a fair-lead for your mooring and anchor lines.

If you know these four knots *well*, you can depend on them for just about everything. They are easy to tie, they hold, they are easy to untie.

This is the ANCHOR BEND. It is used to bend (or fasten) a line to a ring.

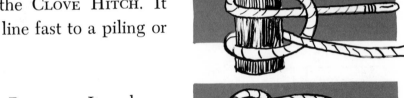

This is the CLOVE HITCH. It makes a line fast to a piling or timber.

This is a BOWLINE. It makes a good, secure loop.

This is a CLEAT. It makes a line fast to a cleat.

Always untie a knot when you have finished using it. Knots left in, weaken a line.

A square knot is handy for tying two lines together, so it's another useful one to know.

DOCKING

It's a good idea to practice docking away from a dock.

Anchor a life ring or other float, and practice coming at it from all sides. Learn how the wind and current affect your boat when you are docking. How does your motor behave if you have to stand off and wait for another boat?

When you are coming into a dock, head into the wind and current, or into whichever is stronger, if they are different.

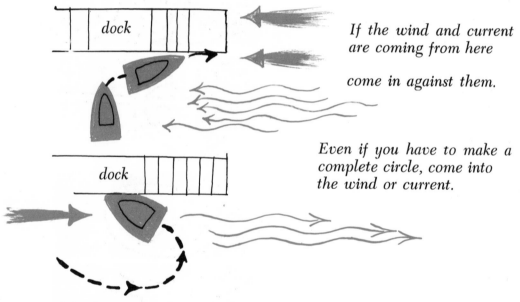

If the wind and current are coming from here

come in against them.

Even if you have to make a complete circle, come into the wind or current.

This slows you down and gives you better control.
Come in slowly, at an angle, bow first.

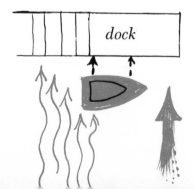

If the wind is blowing straight toward the dock, parallel the dock, then drift in.

50

If you seem to be coming into the dock too fast, reverse your engine.

Have your bow line fastened and ready to cast.

Have fenders ready on the dock side of the boat.

If no one is on the dock to take your line, come alongside, step out with your bow line, tie it, then tie your stern line. Use a clove hitch if there are pilings, a cleat if there are cleats.

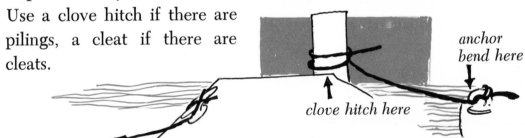

anchor bend here

clove hitch here

When you are mooring onto a dock or float, allow enough line for changes in the tide, the motion of the waves, and the wakes of other boats.

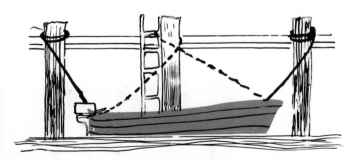

A bow and a stern line are usually enough for a small boat. For extra security, add a center line. Be sure to use enough line to allow for a tide drop!

51

ANCHORING

If you haven't room for two anchors, choose the type most suitable for your local waters.

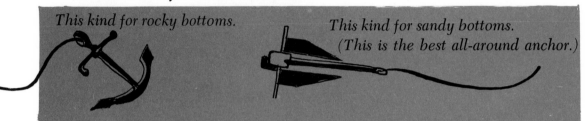

This kind for rocky bottoms.

This kind for sandy bottoms.
(This is the best all-around anchor.)

And be sure your anchor is heavy enough to hold your boat.

When you are anchoring, don't pick a spot so shallow that you'll be aground when the tide goes out. Don't pick a place so deep your anchor can't dig in, with plenty of line to spare.

Be sure that the line is long and strong enough to anchor your boat. Always check the knot that bends the line to the anchor.

Don't anchor too close to other boats. Allow enough clearance for a full circle swing of your boat and those around you if the wind or current changes.

When you are anchoring, come up into the wind or current, whichever is stronger. Lower your anchor; don't throw it.

To anchor properly, so that your anchor will hold in *any* emergency, use at least six times as much line as the water you are anchored in. Here's a handy way to measure your line approximately as you let it down. A fullgrown sailor's arms, outstretched, measure about a fathom, or six feet.

When your anchor touches bottom, let out six times that much line. If you anchor offshore often, you'll find it convenient to mark your anchor line off in lengths.

Does so much line seem silly? A long line doesn't jerk at the boat, and allows the anchor to bite in deeply. If the anchor drags, your boat could bump into other boats, or even float off.

When you feel the anchor bite in, set it by slowly reversing your motor so that you back away. Never cut your motor until the anchor is set.

When you are pulling up, moving slowly ahead over the anchor makes it easier to lift. If the anchor is stuck, try a *slow* circle around it, under power, keeping the line taut.

If the anchor is muddy, rinse it off before you stow it. Coil the anchor line where it can dry.

Whether you are anchoring or pulling up, keep a sharp eye on the distance between your anchor line and your propeller. If you foul your propeller with your anchor line, you go to the foot of the class!

RAFTING

When you are rafting, or tying onto another boat, come alongside as you would to a dock, heading into the wind or current.

Have your lines ready to hand aboard the other boat.

Have fenders out before you tie on. Anchor *before* you tie on.

BEACHING YOUR BOAT

Rowboats, canoes, catamarans, and most outboards can safely be run up onto a beach while you swim or have a picnic. But you have to be careful. Pick a sandy place, not a rocky one. Come in slowly, and if you have an outboard on, either lift your motor at the last minute or be sure there is plenty of water for it. Watch the tide. If it is going out, you may find yourself high and dry. If it is coming in, you might have to swim back to the boat.

If you plan to be on the beach for any length of time, move your boat every now and then, down toward an outgoing tide, up away from an incoming one. But whatever the tide, always put your anchor in the beach.

BOATING IN SPECIAL PLACES

OFFSHORE

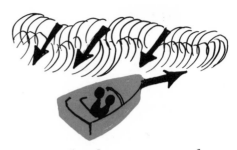

Certainly no one should go "out to sea" in a little motor boat. But sometimes, even in a big sound or bay, the sea gets unexpectedly rough and heavy, and you should know what to do until you can get into harbor.

Meet headseas at an angle, not straight on.

If you are running into big waves in front of the boat—this is called a headsea—meet them at a slight angle instead of head on. It is important also to reduce speed.

The dip between the waves is called the trough. Running in the trough of a heavy sea will make your boat roll, so steer a zig-zag course, like this.

no   *yes*

When the waves are big behind the boat—this is called a following sea—they may throw the boat around or make it "yaw." You are probably going too fast. If you slow down and let the waves pass under you, you'll be safer and steadier.

If you are running for shore and have to come into a strange inlet through a rough sea, remember that every third wave is usually the biggest. Count a few to be sure; then come in *after* a big one.

NOW!

RIVERS

Rivers are fun to explore in a small boat. Here are some things to remember, if you're a river pilot.

In a river or a stream, a boat can be handled best against the current. If you are going with the current, you must go faster than it does or you can't steer. Never drift with a strong current, because then you are out of control.

When a channel narrows, the current increases; when it widens, the current decreases.

SHALLOW

DEEP

SHALLOW

SHALLOW

The deep water in a river is usually darker in color. Where the river is straight, it is usually deepest in the middle. Where the river bends, the deep water is usually on the *outside* of the bend.

Shallow water looks lighter and more ripply, but a really flat, calm patch is probably very, very shallow.

Swirls or patches of rough water usually mean that there are rocks below the surface.

Where other streams come in, sand bars are likely to build up.

swirls show rocks

CANALS

Boating in a canal is fun, but coming through a lock is a tricky business. If possible, raft onto a larger boat that is going through too. You need lots of fenders to come through a lock without getting badly bumped.

LAKES

Very big lakes are like the open sea, and you handle your boat the way you would in coastal waters. But lesser lakes are usually much calmer, and a wonderful place for small boats.

Some lakes have laws against motorboats. If you are trailering your boat, be sure to check before putting it into a strange lake.

Often lakes run into one another, and you can take a fine trip through a chain of lakes. Sometimes, though, there are portages, places where you have to carry the boat overland for a few yards or more. Check for these before you take a lake trip in anything heavier than a canoe or a light powerboat.

Lake water is usually deep until you get fairly close to shore. But near shore, watch for rocks and submerged stumps. And don't forget the insect repellent!

Unpack your canoe before you carry it. Make a second trip for your gear.

WHAT MAKES BOATING ACCIDENTS?

Some boating accidents are caused by bad weather or bad sea conditions, but you can almost always foresee these things. Don't go out in threatening weather, strong winds, or rough water. Even if you are planning to be out for only a few minutes, check the weather report.

Some boating accidents are caused by unsafe boats.

Is the boat leaky?

Is the motor too big, or in bad condition, or not running right?

Most boating accidents are caused by people.

The United States Coast Guard keeps a record of boating accidents and why they happened. Do any of these descriptions fit you?

CAUSES of BOATING ACCIDENTS

CAUSE	RESULT	
	DEATHS	INJURED

The operator of this boat was:
going too fast
loading improperly
fueling improperly
ignorant of the rules of the road
ignorant of safety precautions
ignorant of navigation aids
in a strange area, without a chart
used poor judgment
was reckless
didn't listen to warnings

THESE THINGS REALLY HAPPENED

Boating accidents aren't just stories you read or hear. They *really* happen to *real* people. Here are four of the hundreds of boating accidents that really happen every year.

A family of six went out for a spin in an outboard runabout, on a rough and overcast day. The boat hit a rock that they couldn't see in the waves, and turned over. Because the engine was too big, it dragged the stern down so that only the bow was above the water. The life preservers were locked in a compartment, and nobody had the key. Because of the bad weather, there were no other boats around. After awhile, the father swam off for help and disappeared. The mother and two of the children hung on as long as they could, then sank, one by one. Two girls clung to the bow for four hours until a boat passing, just at dusk, saw them and rescued them. WHAT WOULD YOU HAVE DONE DIFFERENTLY?

A group of teenagers, clowning around in a very fast, flat speedboat, on a lake, fastened the wheel so the boat would run in circles. The wake of another boat tipped them into the water, where their own boat continued to race through them, injuring them all. WHAT WOULD YOU HAVE DONE DIFFERENTLY?

Two men and a boy went out for "an hour's fishing" in an outboard cruiser, before breakfast. They didn't bother to take food, water, or spare gas. A heavy fog rolled in, they got lost, and ran until their gas gave out. Two days later, the boat was found, drifting. The boy was alive, but the men had both died of thirst. WHAT WOULD YOU HAVE DONE DIFFERENTLY?

Two girls, in a small sailboat, were caught in a sudden squall. They took down sail and anchored, but when the boat filled with water they got panicky and decided to swim for shore. Both drowned. When searchers found the boat, still safely anchored and floating, it was in water so shallow that the girls could have walked to land. WHAT WOULD YOU HAVE DONE DIFFERENTLY?

TO THE RESCUE!

These are all distress signals:

any constant horn, bell, or whistle;

the American flag or ensign flying upside down;

someone waving a flag, shirt, *anything*;

a white cloth flying from the highest point of the boat;

any smoke or flare;

a light, blinking SOS—3 short, 3 long, 3 short;

the emergency word "Mayday."

One of the first laws of boating is to help the other fellow. If you see an accident or a distress signal, go immediately and offer help.

BUT

Don't put yourself in danger
and don't get in the way of rescue operations by others who
are doing the job well.

When you are going to the rescue of people in the water,
get life preservers ready on the way. Be sure they are securely
attached to lines.

*Attach lines to
life preservers.*

*Keep
watching!*

Never take your eyes off the people in the water.

Anyone who seems tired or in trouble needs your help *first*.

Come alongside slowly, into the wind or current. Put your
motor in neutral so the propeller stops, but do *not* stop the
motor until the person is within reach. If the current is swift
he may drift away and you will waste valuable time starting
your motor again.

Come alongside slowly.

*Put the motor in
neutral, but
DON'T STOP IT!*

Heave a life preserver, tied to a line, and pull the person over the stern or bow of the boat, balancing it so it will not tip when someone crawls aboard.

If you're pulling someone over the stern, watch that hot motor! And be sure your propeller isn't moving!

DON'T OVERLOAD!

If there are several people in the water, take aboard those who need help most, and tow the others slowly behind on securely fastened lines. There will probably be other boats in the vicinity to take on additional passengers.

If you are towing another boat, fasten its bowline securely to a cleat on the side of your boat, instead of at the stern, if this is possible. You will be able to steer better this way. If the water is rough, use a long tow line. The boat you are pulling should ride on the crest of the wave following you, not in the trough. Travel slowly.

HELP! HELP!

No matter how careful you are, some day you might find yourself in a situation where you need help.

If you are out of gas (you shouldn't be), or your motor won't work (it should, if you keep it in good shape), then all you need is a tow. Show a distress signal and wait until someone comes. (It is good boat manners to hand a rescuing boat *your* line to tow with.)

But if your boat swamps, or turns over, the situation is different. Everyone aboard is in danger, and this calls for cool heads.

The most important thing to remember is

STAY WITH THE BOAT!

If your boat has the proper flotation material, it will float and support you, even if it is filled with water, and it will support you even if it has turned over. Even if the stern is dragged down and you have only a few inches of bow to hang on to, stay with it.

Even part of a boat is easier to see than a swimmer.

Don't try to swim for shore. It's farther than it looks. And the boat is easier to see in the water than you are. Rescuers will find you faster.

You should have a clear, emergency procedure to follow.

1. First count noses to make sure everyone is accounted for. **2.** Then make sure that everyone has a place to hold on to the hull. If someone is hurt, the others will have to support him against it.

Of course all non-swimmers are wearing life preservers.

If the other life preservers were loose in the boat, they may **3.** be floating around you. Catch them, and see that each person has one to support him.

64

If the life preservers are in a compartment, or are trapped
under the boat, the best swimmer goes for them, and someone
else should always be touching him. Whenever you are afloat,
that compartment door should always be ajar, and *never* locked.

4.

When everyone has a life preserver, look for whatever lines
are within reach, and fasten everyone to the boat, in any way
you can. This is easier than holding on to a slippery hull.

5.

Now signal with whatever means you have. On any good
boating day—and you shouldn't be out on any other kind—
rescue should be only a few minutes away.

6.

When you are being rescued, keep calm. See that those who
need help first are rescued first. Do whatever you can to help
the rescuers.

7.

OTHER EMERGENCIES
Fog

If you've kept your weather eye open, you should be ashore long before any fog gets so thick that you can't see your way. But if you are caught, stop, anchor, and wait it out. Otherwise you may run into something, or go in circles until your gas is gone.

Sound your horn or whistle at least one long blast a minute, and keep sounding it, or someone may run into you.

Out After Dark

You should never be out after dark unless you are in an area that is completely familiar to you, and with other boats all around.

Be sure your running lights are on. (Check these on pages 76-77.)

Proceed into harbor slowly, using your chart of the area. The lights, bells, and lighted buoys are marked on the chart. They should show you your exact position and where the channel is, like this:

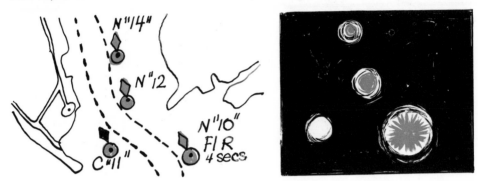

SUDDEN STORMS

No matter how sudden a storm is, it shouldn't catch you napping. But if you *are* out, and the water gets rough, remember how we talked on page 55 about handling the waves. Meet headseas at a slight angle;
run zig-zag instead of in the trough;
don't go too fast in a following sea, but let it run under you.

If the storm is bad, stop and anchor if you can, or put out a sea anchor (page 30). And remember, even if the boat swamps, *stay with it!*

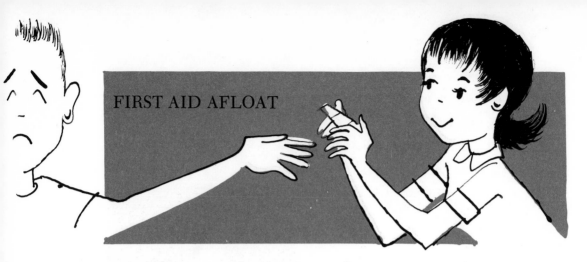

FIRST AID AFLOAT

Accidents can happen anywhere. But on a boat, it isn't always possible to get help right away. It's important to have a first aid kit aboard, and to know what to do in an emergency.

The greatest emergency aboard would probably be a near-drowning. Remember, A PERSON IS NOT NECESSARILY DEAD BECAUSE HE ISN'T BREATHING. But you must help him to get air right away, by breathing for him.

Rescue breathing is blowing air into a person through his mouth or nose, and then letting the air come out.

Don't waste a moment. The person may die.

Don't try to get him to shore, or go for help.

Start the instant you reach him, even if he is still in the water, even while he is being pulled into the boat. Don't stop to drain the water out.

RESCUE BREATHING WORKS THIS WAY

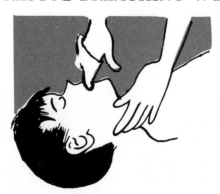

Wipe away, with your fingers wrapped in cloth, anything that you can see in the victim's mouth that doesn't belong there.

Tilt his head back as far as possible.

Open your mouth wide and take a deep breath.

Seal your mouth around his and blow in, closing off his nostrils by pressing your cheek against them.

Take your mouth away, turn your head to the side, and listen for the air to come rushing back.

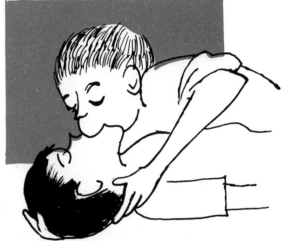

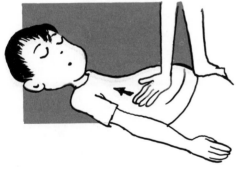

Repeat this fast for the first ten breaths; then slow down to 10-20 breaths a minute. (If he begins to look bulgy from too much air inside, press his belly to push the air out.)

Don't stop until he starts breathing by himself, and start again if he should stop. You can rescue breathe for hours if you have to.

Rescue breathing is not just for drowning. You can use it in any accident in which a person stops breathing.

OTHER FIRST AID

SHOCK

Any time some one has been in an accident, even if he is not hurt, he will suffer from shock. Shock can be very dangerous by itself. A person in shock will be very pale, perspiring, with clammy hands and feet.

Lay him down, with his feet higher than his head.

Don't let him get chilled. If the day is cool, he needs additional clothing or blankets.

If he is conscious, give him something hot to drink.

Talk to him calmly, and keep him from getting excited. Don't move him unnecessarily.

Whenever someone is dizzy, or loses consciousness, the color of his face tells you what to do:

Face red, raise the head,

Face pale, raise the tail. (Feet, really, but that doesn't rhyme!)

SUNBURN, HEAT PROSTRATION

The sun is much more potent on the water, because it is reflected, too. Don't spend a sunny day on a boat dressed in a bathing suit, unless you are *very* brown. Apply a suntan preparation often. If you have a bad sunburn, avoid getting chilled.

face red. . . .

face pale. . . .

Sometimes too much sun and heat can cause heat prostration. A person suffering from heat prostration gets dizzy, and very red in the face. Lying down, head higher than the feet, helps. Loosen clothing, and splash cool water on the face.

In hot weather, loose, comfortable, light-colored clothes are best to wear for a day's boating.

SEASICKNESS

You shouldn't be out in really rough, rolling water, but some people get sick even when it's calm. Anyone subject to seasickness should take seasick pills before starting out. Keep seasick pills in your first aid kit. Fresh air helps, so don't go below, even if there is a cabin with a bunk.

FISH HOOKS

If you are fishing from a boat, be careful of those flying fish hooks. Never cast across the boat.

If someone gets hooked, and the hook is in past the barb, you can't pull it out the way it went in. (The barb was made that way to keep the fish from pulling loose.) Get the patient to a doctor as fast as you can, and let him do the job.

MINIMUM FLOATING FIRST AID KIT

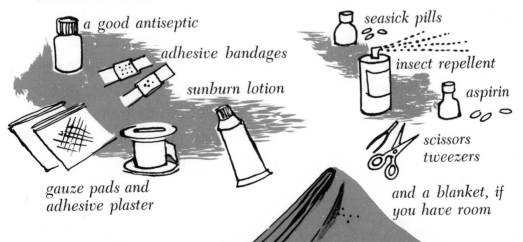

a good antiseptic

adhesive bandages

sunburn lotion

gauze pads and adhesive plaster

seasick pills

insect repellent

aspirin

scissors
tweezers

and a blanket, if you have room

71

You should be able to swim for ten minutes, fully dressed.

SWIMMING

Every sailor should know how to swim. Being sure of yourself in the water will make you more relaxed on top of it, and much cooler-headed in an emergency. You should swim well enough to take care of yourself and others, if they need help.

If you are swimming from a beach, always swim near shore and away from boating channels. It is almost impossible for the driver of a boat to see a swimmer among the waves and wakes of the channel. Swimming there is just plain dangerous.

If you want to swim from your boat, never anchor it in or near the channel, but in an anchorage near shore and near other anchored boats. Never swim alone from your boat. Someone should be swimming with you, or be aboard, watching. Never dive from a boat unless you know how deep the water is, or if there are rocks on the bottom.

Except in an emergency, don't swim directly after a meal.

When you are swimming from a boat always keep a line floating out behind. Tie one end securely to the stern cleat and tie a life ring to the other. It makes a handy thing to grab if you get tired, or if the current is stronger than you thought.

72

Distances on water can fool you. If your boat ever turns over, grab a life preserver, swim to the boat, and hold on. Even if you are a strong swimmer, *don't* try to swim for shore. It's almost always farther than it looks.

SKIN DIVING

Skin diving is not a learn-by-trying sport. A beginning skin diver needs lessons from an expert. He also needs proper equipment, properly tested and approved. You wouldn't think of teaching yourself to fly, in an airplane you had assembled yourself. Try-it-and-see skin diving, with haphazard equipment, is just as silly.

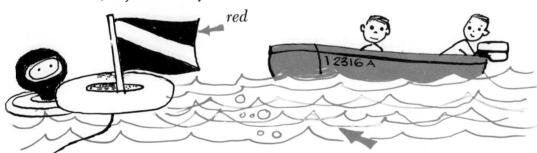

red

If you are in a boat and you see this flag, it means a skin diver is there. Unless your motor is off, do not approach within 100 feet, and go slowly anywhere in the area. If you see bubbles, don't pass over them. Remember, too, skin divers never dive alone, so keep your eyes open for two or more.

The driver watches the boat.
The observer watches the skier.

WATER SKIING

Water skiing is a team sport, and there must be at least three people on the team. In most places it is a law that the skier and the driver have to be assisted by an observer in the boat. The observer's job is to watch the skier and pass his signals to the driver, to watch the tow rope and the boat's wake.

It takes extra boating skill to drive for a water skier. It is harder to maneuver a boat while towing, and of course you must still obey the rules of the road. When you are driving, leave the skier to the observer, and give all your attention to the boat.

Remember that it is dangerous to the skier to turn the boat sharply. Make big, wide turns, keeping the skier inside the wake.

A ski rope must be at least 75 feet long. To be safe, you have to keep the skier at least twice that distance from other boats, docks, and swimmers. Remember that you could be guilty of recklessness or negligence if you go faster than 5 miles an hour within 100 feet of docks, swimmers, beaches, or anchorages. A skier would sink at that speed.

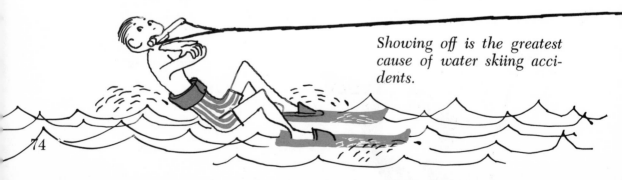

Showing off is the greatest cause of water skiing accidents.

When a skier falls, circle *slowly* back to him, then around him, so he can catch the towline again. If you are going to bring him aboard, be sure the motor is in neutral so *the propeller is not turning.*

Let him board at bow or stern, whichever is safer. Watch the propeller and the hot motor. Then pick up the skis.

Never water ski when it is dark. In most places it is against the law.

The skier should control the boat. Don't try to fool him or outguess him.

The skier, the observer, and the driver should know and use these signals:

turn right

turn left

faster

slower

speed's fine

cut the motor

whip off

stop

back to the dock

CHECKLIST OF BOATING LAWS

Every state has its own boating laws. You should be familiar with those of your state and those of any neighboring state where you cruise. But there is also a Federal Boating Act, which affects all boats all over the country. It says that:

Every pleasure boat of more than 10 horsepower must have a number, and be registered either in its own state or with the federal government if there is no state registration law approved by the Coast Guard.

The operator of any boat involved in an accident *must* stop and give assistance. If someone is hurt, or the damage is greater than $100, the accident must be reported. Usually your local police or Coast Guard station can give you a form to fill out and tell you where to send it.

Operators must exchange names and addresses, and identify their boats.

Everywhere, the operator of a boat is responsible for any damage caused by the wake of his boat.

Every boat, big or small, if it is out after sunset, must have running lights.

Boats under 26 feet should have lights like this:

POWER BOATS

These lights are correct only for Inland Waters, Western Rivers, and the Great Lakes.

white, 32 point, visible for 2 miles

combination red and green, 20 point, 1 mile

POWER BOATS

These lights are correct for all waters—Inland, Coastal, and International.

white, 12 point, 2 miles

white, 20 point, 3 miles

combination red and green, 20 point, 1 mile

A 32 pt. (point) light shows all around the horizon

20 pt. combination light

12 pt. light

It's a good idea to check these laws in your own area:

Do you need an adult aboard?

Must you have a safety certificate if you are under 14?

In what waters are all powerboats forbidden?

Must you register your outboard motor?

Are there speed limits, even if they are not posted?

Boating laws are simple, everywhere. A good boatman knows that by being careful, courteous, and responsible he can help to keep them that way.

SAIL AND POWER

white all around, 2 miles

combination red and green, 20 point, 1 mile

SAIL ONLY

flashlight or flare

red and green, 20 point, 1 mile

SAIL AND POWER

white, 12 point, 2 miles

white, 20 point, 3 miles

red and green, 20 point, 1 mile

SAIL ONLY

white, 12 point, 2 miles

red and green, 20 point, 1 mile

SOME RULES FOR GOOD BOATMEN

Never hurry or be careless. A good seaman is workmanlike.

Never overload your boat.

Keep a weather eye open.

Learn to swim. A swimmer is at ease on or in the water, and isn't likely to panic.

Never use a boat in dangerous or off-limit waters, and be extra-careful in unfamiliar waters.

Know your boat.

Know and obey the rules of the road.

INDEX

80